"Extrapolating the nuances of what it means to be a girl in 2018, Melody Pourmoradi's book *XOXO, from a girl who gets it: Life notes for the young girl within*, really hits the nail on the head. An absolute must read for the girl that needs a push toward confidence and a guide to commanding respect. Buy it for your daughter, sister, niece, mom, every woman in your life that needs a pick me up."
—**IMAN OUBOU, FOUNDER AND CEO OF SWAAY MEDIA**

"I like *XOXO, from a girl who gets it: Life notes for the young girl within*, because it's uplifting and I get to read it with my mommy. I like how it teaches about giving compliments, being kind, and helping! And I LOVE the pictures!"
—**MAYA LE CLARK, ACTRESS ON NICKELODEON'S "THE THUNDERMANS"**

"Melody Pourmoradi is a true gem, who has made it her mission to empower young girls to believe in themselves and to always follow their heart. Her book *XOXO, from a girl who gets it: Life notes for the young girl within* is a compilation of wisdom and insight that all girls can relate to regardless of age. Her authenticity and enthusiastic nature shines through her positive messages and has a way of getting you to realize that everything you need is right inside of you. I wish I had a book like this when I was growing up to support me in my life journey!"
—**DIANA ALVARADO, GIRLIFE FACILITATOR**

"*XOXO, from a girl who gets it: Life notes for the young girl within*, can help girls realize their talents and abilities and encourages them to explore their inner-power. Every young girl deserves the chance to discover what makes them special."
—**VICKI SAUNDERS, FOUNDER OF SheEO**

XOXO,
from a girl who gets it

Life notes for the young girl within

Melody Pourmoradi

www.LifeEvolutionsCoaching.com

GIRLLIFE™
www.LifeEvolutionsCoaching.com

Illustrations © 2018 Debbie Hernandez
Text © 2018 Melody Pourmoradi

10 9 8 7 6 5 4 3 2

First Edition 2018

ISBN: 978-1-7320980-0-8

This book is dedicated to my loving husband Navid
and to my daughters Ella & Noa who are and
continue to be my greatest teachers.
I love you with all my heart.

To my supportive family and friends and all of
the incredibly strong women in my life
(you know who you are), thank you for
your example and for your grace.

INTRODUCTION

Hello and welcome, Brilliant Girl, I'm so glad you're here!

You, me, and all the other girls and women out there are so unbelievably lucky to be part of the female family. As girls and women, we have a special brand of magic that enables us to raise each other up, transform our world, and shine brighter and brighter each day.

A little about me:

As a young girl growing up, I so often struggled to feel important, smart, and beautiful. Sometimes it is hard to find those things in a world where people seem to be comparing you to everyone else and trying to turn you into their idea of what it is to be "a good girl" or "a pretty girl." You know what I mean? I've worked really hard to find my *own* inner beauty and to trust my *own* inner wisdom, and I've made it my mission to help other girls and women do same. And you know what? It feels so good to share the love! In this book, I share many different ingredients that will help you create a life recipe that is as special and unique as you are. No two recipes will be the same, which is precisely what makes each one so special. The most important ingredient in changing my own life for the better was choosing positive thoughts that made me feel good from the inside out. You see, once I learned that I could actually choose my own thoughts—specifically ones that make me feel happy, free, and at peace—my whole entire world changed for the better.

A little about you:

I want you to know that you too can find your *own* way to feel good and to see the best in the world around you. The best part is that everything you need to live a life beyond your wildest dreams is already inside of you. Yup, it's the truth! My intention in writing this book is to help you uncover your own unique strengths and gifts, and to help you to see all of those things in others too.

Each of the messages in this book will help you to discover all of the wisdom and power that have already been in your heart all of this time. You can either read this book from start to finish, or you can close your eyes and randomly pick a page. I am confident that each of these messages will be exactly what you need to hear at this very moment. Here's the thing—the most important part about making new ideas real is to actually *do* them. At the end of each note, I will ask you a question about how you can bring these ideas into your life. Do your best each day to find your own answers so that you can go through each moment feeling comfortable and peaceful. Can you promise to try?

A little about us:

I wrote this book, beautiful one, with you in mind. If you are a woman who is ready to hear the wisdom that the young girl within you so longs to hear, I hope this book speaks to you. If you are a young girl on a journey to discovering all of the beauty and brilliance that is bubbling up inside of you, I hope this book inspires you. If you are a mother who wants to raise an empowered girl to know how innately strong she is, I hope this book supports you.

I really believe the good things are better when shared, so go ahead...invite your friend, your sister, your mother, or your daughter and enjoy reading these messages together. There is a hashtag at the end of each note so feel free to snap a shot of one of the illustrations that really speaks to you and tell us what you love about it. On social media use the hashtag provided along with my favorite hashtag, #xoxofromagirl so that we can stay connected and I can see how you are enjoying the book too.

You are magic, my love, pure magic, and I can't wait for you to find all the ways that *you* (and only you) light up this world.

Here's to feeling empowered together. Let's do this thing! #wevegotthis

you have the power to get through anything

Hey, Resilient Girl,

You are powerful beyond measure. Did you know that? You were born with the strength and skill to get through every difficult experience that life might throw your way. Think of one of the obstacles in your life that you never thought you would make it through. Guess what? Not only did you get through it, but you came out of the experience as a stronger person. That's the power that I'm talking about. All you have to do is believe in that power, and it will grow more and more each day. So from here on in, instead of breaking because of tough situations, I want you to imagine yourself bending like an elastic band does; it stretches and comes back stronger than ever. How can you choose to stand in your power right now, in the midst of a difficult situation in your life? #powerup

XOXO,

from a girl who gets it

Hey, Dazzling Girl,

Did you know that every thought that you think creates the kind of life that you live? It's kind of like a choose-your-own-adventure book where the final outcome is in your hands. Every thought creates a feeling in your mind and body so if you want to feel good, it's super important that you choose thoughts that raise you up. You know, the ones that make you feel proud, strong, and powerful. The next time you are feeling down, ask yourself: "What thought am I thinking that's making me feel so low?" Once you have figured it out—and I know you will!—all you have to do is choose another thought that energizes and excites you. You always have the power to choose a new thought. What's one positive thought that you can choose to think right this second? #thoughtpower

XOXO,
from a girl who gets it

Hello, Wonderful Girl,

This may be news to you, but here it goes... Whatever is going on in your life, you have the power to make your own choices. You can choose how to respond to a mean person. You can choose how to feel in every moment. You can choose what thoughts to think. You can choose what kind of friends you surround yourself with. You can choose what foods to feed your body with. Have I made myself clear? Along with your ability to choose comes a personal responsibility to accept the outcomes of your choices. So please, in every moment of your life, choose wisely and thoughtfully. Make every effort to learn from choices that didn't end so well and celebrate the choices that did. What's one choice you made in the past that you can learn from? #itsyourchoice

XOXO,
from a girl who gets it

☆ BE REAL ☆
(A HOW-TO GUIDE)

Don't try to be a people pleaser

Follow your own style

Express your individuality

Surround yourself with positive people

Don't worry about what others think of you

Be open and honest with yourself

Hey, Sweet Soul,

All the world really wants from you is for you to be your truest, real-est self. I know that sometimes we act differently to fit in or be accepted by a certain group of people—I've totally been there. The thing is, though, that if you try to be "somebody else," you will attract friends into your life who like that "somebody else," not the real and amazing you. It doesn't feel good to pretend for the sake of others. Be honest with yourself... How long can you keep that kind of game up, anyway? Maybe the most interesting and exciting thing about you is the thing you are most afraid to share. How unfair would it be to you and to the world to not experience the real you? It would be a straight-up shame! What's one very real thing about you that makes you fabulous? #getreal

XOXO,
from a girl who gets it

Hey, Glow Girl,

When I was young, I thought that we were either born with smarts or we weren't. As I got older, I started to realize that each of us is brilliant in our own way. Kind of like the stars in the sky, each brilliant, yet each so different from one another. You have a special gift to give the world by sharing the things that come to you naturally from your heart. Remember that we all have strengths and weaknesses, and if we compare our smarts to somebody else's, we will always find a way to feel like we are not enough. Shine bright girl, and know that your brand of intelligence is unique and so needed on our planet. What's one thing about you that makes you feel brilliant? #ownyourbrilliance

XOXO,

from a girl who gets it

Note #6

Hello Unique Girl,

It's really important to me and to the entire world that you know how special and wonderful you truly are. You play a one-of-a-kind role in the lives of so many people, and the world simply wouldn't be the same if you weren't born. Kind of like a missing puzzle piece from a big, beautiful masterpiece. You are worthwhile and so valuable simply because you are alive. Always remember what a perfect creation you are. You are the light of the world, brilliant girl. Don't be afraid to shine. How does it feel to know that your presence is so significant for so many? #youmatter

XOXO,
from a girl who gets it

Hey, Sensitive Girl,

It's okay to sometimes not feel okay. Life isn't always going to be rainbows and unicorns. There will be times when you feel down, hurt, angry, or out-of-control. Sometimes you will even experience all of the emotions at the same time! It's totally natural to have many different emotions. That's what makes you a human being. Allow yourself to feel what you feel so that you can face it and move on. Just promise me one thing: it's very important that you always find a way to help yourself feel better after you made the effort to really feel your emotions. Got it? What's one way that you can get through something that's upsetting you right now? #feelitfirst

XOXO,
from a girl who gets it

Note #8

Hello, Beautiful Girl,

Did you know that in any situation, simply taking a deep breath can be your lifeline? When you are feeling nervous, fearful, or anxious, find a quiet place inside of you and take a few deep breaths. Doing this can calm you down and make you feel yourself again. When you breathe in, imagine bringing in the things that make you smile. When you breathe out, let go of anything you no longer want to think about. Notice your breath right at this moment. Is it short and tight, or is it slow and comfortable? Take every opportunity today to tune into your breathing and create peace in your body. Can you take a moment today to stop and breathe deeply? #breatheitout

XOXO,
from a girl who gets it

THROW AWAY YOUR EXCUSES

Note #9

Dear Incredible Girl,

For everything that you want to be, achieve, and create in your life, you will always be able to find an excuse, if that's what you choose to look for. Don't seek out the excuses, because they will only stop you from doing, being, and having what you want. Instead, make a promise to yourself to notice all the reasons that you can accomplish your goal and let that unstoppable energy guide your every move. What's one excuse you are willing to let go of to finally do that thing you've been wanting to do? #excusefree

XOXO,

from a girl who gets it

Choose friends who are partners-in-Shine

Hey, Darling Girl,

The friends that you surround yourself with can make an enormous difference in how you feel. Did you know that we start behaving like the people that we spend the most time with? It's a fact! So take this from me, choose friends who make you a better person, you know, the ones who see the best in you and support you unconditionally. Remember that it's a two-way street, so be sure to do the same thoughtful things for them that you would expect them to do for you. When you have healthy friendships, together you can shine, and become the best versions of yourself. Who is one friend that is your partner in shine? #shiningtogether

XOXO,

from a girl who gets it

You have the power to heal yourself

(what do you need right now?)

A warm tea

time with a cute animal

A long walk

Exercise

a deep breath

A friend to talk to

A good book

time to make something

A big hug

Note #11

Hiya, Healthy Girl,

You know those times when you are feeling sick, sad, or uncomfortable? I have discovered that inside of us is everything that we need to feel better fast. When I was younger, I thought I had to run to mom, the doctor, or anybody (other than myself) to figure out how to heal. Now I know that the best thing to do at times like this is to check in with myself and ask, "What do I need right now?" Sometimes for me, the answer is a warm cup of tea, a deep breath, or a friend to talk to. Now, of course I'm not talking about the times when there is an emergency or something that requires the help of an adult or professional. I'm talking about the day-to-day stuff that sometimes gets us in a funk. It's important to know the difference. You know what I mean? The next time you are feeling down in the dumps, simply ask this very important question: "What do I need right now?" #youcanhealyourself

XOXO,
from a girl who gets it

I am responsible for the WORLD I see

(choose your outlook)

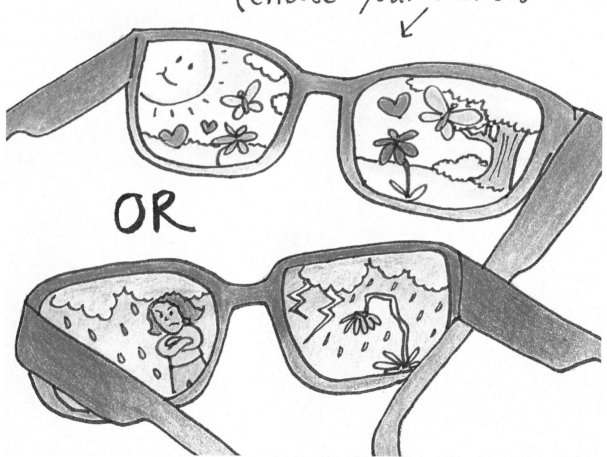

OR

Note #12

Hey, Special Girl,

You know what? Your outlook totally shapes how you see the world and how you feel all the time. If you blame other people and other circumstances for the things that are going wrong in your life, then you are making a choice to give your power away. Once you give up your power, you have given up your role in changing the situation for the better. What's really cool about all of this is that if you actually take responsibility for the things that you can change, then your power grows. Remember that you always get to choose. What's one way that you have been giving your power away by blaming? How can you choose to change that right now? #blamenomore

XOXO,
from a girl who gets it

Your opinion of yourself is more important than anyone else's opinion of you.

Note #13

Hey, Soul Sister,

Do you ever get so wrapped up in what others think of you that you totally forget how you want to be and who you want to be? I beg of you to do your best to stop this immediately! Because you know what? What other people think of you is none of your business. What you think of you is the most important because you are the one living your life. Make every effort to do things that make you feel good about yourself. What's one thing you can do today that you will be proud of? #proudofme

XOXO,

from a girl who gets it

DONT BELIEVE EVERYTHING YOU SEE ON SOCIAL MEDIA

Liked by Mom and
4 others

124 likes

Before

- Natural skin
- bad lighting
- No filter

After

- Smoothed out skin with editing
- flattering lighting
- filter added

Note #14

Hey, Admirable Girl,

You know what? The pictures you see on Instagram/Snapchat/Facebook are not always showing you what's real. Have you ever posted a picture of yourself when you're crying or sad or even angry? Neither have I. When we share a photo, we are usually highlighting the good times. Sometimes we just can't help it, but we start to compare our lives to other people's just based on a simple photo that has shown up on our feed—I know the feeling too. I've been there. Comparing ourselves is never going to make us feel good because there will always be someone who seems to have more or less than we do. Got it? And while you're at it, please stop following any accounts in cyberspace that don't elevate or inspire you to be a better person. 'K? The next time you're on social media and you start experiencing feelings of sadness or envy, how can you remind yourself of what is real? #fomofree

XOXO,
from a girl who gets it

Loving Yourself will be one of the most important things you'll ever do

LOVE

YOU

Note #15

Hey, Graceful Girl,

One of your biggest jobs from this day forward is to practice the art of loving yourself. All the things you so often do for others, like complimenting them or getting excited to spend time with them, I want you to start doing for yourself. Self-love is about treating yourself with the respect that you deserve all the time. The kinder you are to you, the better everything in your life becomes. This includes your friendships, your mood, and your ability to have fun. So from this day forward, treat yourself and talk to yourself the way you would with someone you love so, so much. You owe yourself the love you so easily give to others. At the end of the day, take it from me, the most important relationship in your life is the one that you have with yourself. What's one thing you can do today show yourself some love? #selfloverules

XOXO,

from a girl who gets it

FAILURE IS ONE OF YOUR GREATEST TEACHERS
Haven't tried this path yet. Could be the one.
Fell into a patch of itchy plants and ended up in an unfamiliar forest
Got lost for an hour on this path
Lead to an unknown village, had to turn back

Note #16

Hey, Brave Girl,

I know that the word failure can freak you out, which is why I want you to start thinking of it in a new way. Every single time you or I have failed at anything at all, it was proof that we were actually trying. It also taught us how not to do something the next time around. All of the most epic inventions first started with an idea that actually didn't work many, many times—until it finally did. That goes for telephones, TVs, cars, and airplanes too. If the inventors gave up because of the hundred times they failed, there are so many things the world would be missing out on. So, from now on when you fail, I want you to pat yourself on the back for trying and then keep on trying. Don't give too much energy to those failures, because whatever you focus on will grow. Instead, put your attention on the possibility that it will happen. Now that you know what failure really is, what's one failure in your life that wasn't really a failure at all? #failforward

XOXO,
from a girl who gets it

Note #17

Hi, Creative Girl,

Your imagination is one of the strongest superpowers that you have, and the best part is that you can use it every single day to achieve your goals. For example, if you are feeling nervous about doing something, anything, let's say singing for your school recital, you can actually practice in your imagination before you even get there. You see, you've got this great big creation machine in your mind, and all you have to do is create a movie in your brain of how you want everything to happen in real life. Visualize yourself at the concert. What are you singing, what are you are wearing? How are you feeling in that moment? The key is to picture what you want and then to work super hard to actually make it happen. How can you use your imagination to make your wishes come true? #imaginethis

XOXO,

from a girl who gets it

You are most beautiful when you are HAPPY

Note #18

Hello, Joyful Girl,

I believe that happy is the new pretty. When you are truly happy, it really shows. It's like an inner light spreads throughout your body and radiates from the inside out. When you are having a good time, it changes your energy and it transforms the way the people around you feel when they are with you. So if you want to feel happy in your mind and body and share that magnetic energy with the world, find every opportunity to choose happiness in each moment of your life. What's one way that you can shine right now, from the inside out? #happyisthenewpretty

XOXO,
from a girl who gets it

Note #19

Hey, Passionate Girl,

Life is so much more fun when we make the time to do the things we absolutely love! The best way to uncover these talents is to try a lot of new things and be open to new ideas and experiences. You will know your passions when you find them because taking part in them will make you feel like you are exactly where you are supposed to be. Believe in what makes you feel lit up and share it with those around you—the world simply wouldn't be complete if you didn't practice your unique magic. What's one passion that you already know you have? #passionategirl

XOXO,

from a girl who gets it

Everything you need is already inside of you.

Note #20

Hey, Precious Girl,

Take this from me—everything you need and want to feel, you've got to create inside of yourself first. You want people to treat you right? Treat yourself right first. You want people to accept you? Accept yourself first. You want people to notice you? Notice yourself first. Try thinking this way whenever you are searching for something that just doesn't seem to come your way. When you find what you need on the inside first, you become a magnet for happiness and success. You get what I'm saying? Taking care of your own needs is an inside job, so don't go looking anywhere but on the inside to create a life that you love. What's one thing that you are ready to start looking for inside of yourself today? #lookinside

XOXO,
from a girl who gets it

You are born with **SUPERPOWERS**

"My Superpowers"

Fearlessly shares her opinions

Expresses empathy for others

Incredibly self-aware

Always knows how to make others smile or laugh when they're feeling down

Possesses the gift of patience

A trustworthy friend

Note #21

Hey, Super Girl,

I bet you didn't know that you have hundreds of superpowers. It's the truth! We all do. There are unique tools inside of you that help you grow stronger every day. Sometimes you can feel your superpowers from as far back as you can remember, and other times, it will take a really hard experience for you to really know and understand that they are there. Here's the good part: when you actually uncover your superpowers, you can use them as often as you want, and their power grows each time they get used. My superpowers are compassion, kindness, and patience. What are some of yours? #powergirl

XOXO,
from a girl who gets it

Your words create your WORLD
I'll do my best
I GOT THIS
I will get through this
I CAN'T!
WHY ME?
It's NOT FAIR!

Note #22

Hi, Smart Girl,

Did you know that the words that you use each and every day are setting you up to either live an amazing life or a disappointing life? Using words like "I can't," "Why me?" or "It's not fair" only block your creativity and will make you feel like you have no control over your life. It also sends a message of weakness and inability to the people you speak to. Instead, use words like "I'll do my best," "I've got this," or "I will get through this" so that you can take your power back and take ownership of your life. Remember that you always get to choose your words. The words that you choose send a message to yourself and to the people you are having a conversation with. Do you want that message to be a positive one or a negative one? #mywordscreatemyworld

XOXO,

from a girl who gets it

Upgrade from "envy" to ☆ Inspiration ☆

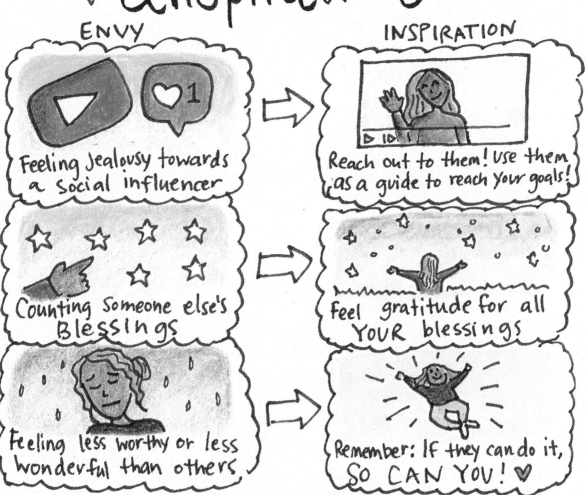

ENVY

INSPIRATION

Feeling jealousy towards a social influencer

Reach out to them! Use them as a guide to reach your goals!

Counting someone else's Blessings

Feel gratitude for all YOUR blessings

Feeling less worthy or less wonderful than others

Remember: If they can do it, SO CAN YOU! ♥

Note #23

Hey, Bright Girl,

You know that icky feeling of envy that sometimes leaves you feeling blocked and alone? We have all experienced it at some point. The next time you find yourself wanting what someone else has, or wanting to be like someone else, remind yourself that you—yes, you—have a certain kind of magic that is all your own. That bright light that you see in your friend, sister, or mom also lives inside of you. Let someone else's success motivate you to go after your own desires and goals. Let their strength be an example of all that is possible for you too in your own special way. How can you be inspired today by someone you admire? #beinspired

XOXO,
from a girl who gets it

Become besties with your ~ INTUITION ~

I'm "Intuition"! Your inner voice that's always looking out for you!

Note #24

Hey, Magical Girl,

Your intuition is that inner voice that often speaks to you when you strongly feel that something is right or it's not. When your intuition is trying to guide you, you feel it in your heart and sometimes even in your entire body too. It's up to you to decide what that inner messenger is trying to communicate with you. This voice can help keep you safe by alerting you that something may be dangerous. It can also share when something excites you and must be explored. Make every effort to tune into your body and mind when that strong feeling inside starts to bubble up, and ask yourself: "What is my intuition trying to share with me and how will I respond?" #intuitiveme

XOXO,

from a girl who gets it

Your Kindness can change the world ♥

(what can you do today?)

Leave a letter in a library book

Compliment a friend

Buy coffee for a stranger

Give someone flowers

Help cook dinner

Volunteer at a soup kitchen

Hello, Loving Girl,

One thing I know for sure is that kindness is the most important ingredient for creating a peaceful and loving world. Always know that your kind words, actions, and wishes have the power to travel throughout our planet and create a giant positive change for us all. I have seen for myself how a loving gesture from one person to another is contagious. Something as simple as a smile or holding the door for someone immediately starts a chain reaction of people helping other people. What I love most about spreading kindness is that it is totally a win-win situation for everyone involved. You will feel so uplifted when you share your goodness with someone and the person who receives your kindness is literally lit up too. What are some opportunities you have today to be kind to those around you? #kindnesscounts

XOXO,

from a girl who gets it

Note #26

Hey, Mindful Girl,

You have absolutely zero control over the things that other people say and do. I know, you wish you did, but you don't. The only person whose actions and feelings you can manage are your own. The next time you find yourself getting angry or sad about something outside of yourself, repeat this reminder over and over again: "Peace begins with me." This means that no matter what is going on in your outer world, if you truly want to be peaceful and content, you have to find a way to create that peace inside of yourself. I can't tell you how many times these words have saved me when I felt out of control. As we've discussed, the magic is always inside of you. You can't wait for someone else to save you whenever you are down. The power is in your hands to find your own peace. What's one tough situation where the words "peace begins with me" can be helpful to you? #peacebeginswithme

XOXO,
from a girl who gets it

Note #27

Hi, Peaceful Girl,

Did you know that your greatest power is right in this very moment? I know you often think back to the things that happened yesterday and last week, or you are worried about what is going to happen tomorrow and next month. The thing is, you can't change anything that has already passed, and you don't know for sure what tomorrow will bring. The moment that you are in today is the one that matters most, so whenever your mind wanders, remind yourself to come back to enjoy and appreciate where you are right this second. What are some ways that you can bring yourself back when you start to think about yesterday or tomorrow? #beherenow

XOXO,
from a girl who gets it

Be kind to your body

Your nose gives your face character & lets you smell every scent

Your eyes see and appreciate the world

Your arms can give big hugs

Your stomach breaks down food and fights infections

Your legs take you to places far and wide

Why you should love your body

Note #28

Hello, Marvelous Girl,

Your body is a beautiful creation of art. Did you know that? It is growing in exactly the way it is supposed to. Try not to compare your body's changes to somebody else's, because every girl develops in a different way and at a different time. Learn to accept and appreciate the changes in every phase and find things about your body that you love each and every day. When you take care of your body, your body will take care of you. If you ever need to talk to someone about the changes, talk to an older girl or woman that you trust. Don't be shy. We've all been where you are, and we all look back wishing that we had welcomed the changes more. I know it's easy for me to say because I've already been there. What is one thing you love about your body today? #bodypositivity

XOXO,

From a girl who gets it

Your mind and your body are connected

Note #29

Hey, Divine Girl,

Your mind and your body are partners in shine. They are finding ways to communicate with each other all the time without you even noticing. Here's how it works: your brilliant body actually responds to what you think. This means that it is so, so, so important that you get smart about what you allow into your mind. Feed your mind with feel-good thoughts. Your body is totally listening and will become stronger and healthier with every loving thought that you think. And yes, you guessed it, negative thoughts will make you weaker and will lower your energy too, so try to stay away from those. What are some positive thoughts that you can feed your mind right now? #mindbodylove

XOXO,

from a girl who gets it

Embrace change

Note #30

Hey, Growing Girl,

I want you to decide for yourself right now that you will welcome change whenever it shows up in your life. Things are always changing—that's just part of life. Sometimes you will change your mind, and that's totally okay because as you grow and learn more, you will make new decisions. Other times, your circle of friends might change because you are all growing in different directions. Your body will change as you blossom into a stronger and even healthier young lady. The important thing through all these shifts is that you are true to who you are and stay connected to the voice of your heart. What's one change in your life that you are finally ready to accept? #embracechange

XOXO,

from a girl who gets it

Support other Girls

Inspire someone

Support and encourage someone

motivate someone to create and do

Achieve a goal and offer advice

YOU GOT THIS!

FINISH LINE

Note #31

Greetings Generous Girl,

From here on in, I want you to start thinking of other girls as your sisters. I want you to know that together you are much stronger than any of you could ever be apart. You know all those things that you wish for yourself? I want you to start wishing them for her too. Compliment other girls. Collaborate with other girls. Root for other girls. Support other girls. Incredible, in fact, unbelievable things happen when we take each other's hands and remember that we are all in this together. How can you support one of your sisters today? #girlssupportinggirls

XOXO,
from a girl who gets it

Let go of your worries

Blow each of your worries into a bubble, and watch it fly away and pop and disappear...

POP

POP

POP

Note #32

Hey, Courageous Girl,

It's officially time to let go of the worry. Worrying for me was just about the hardest thing I had to get a grip on when I was growing up. I would worry about anything and everything—too many things to name. Here's the thing about worry: that "horrific" event that you are destroying yourself about is almost always a much bigger deal in your mind than in real life. On top of that, once the event is over, whether it was awful or not doesn't even matter because you will forget about it so soon after it even happens (if it happens). Remember what I told you before, your power is always in the present moment, so stop getting wrapped up in something in the future that you simply cannot control. The next time you find yourself in a worry wonderland, remind yourself of our talk here. How can you kick your worry to the curb today? #laterworries

XOXO,
from a girl who gets it

THINK FOR YOURSELF

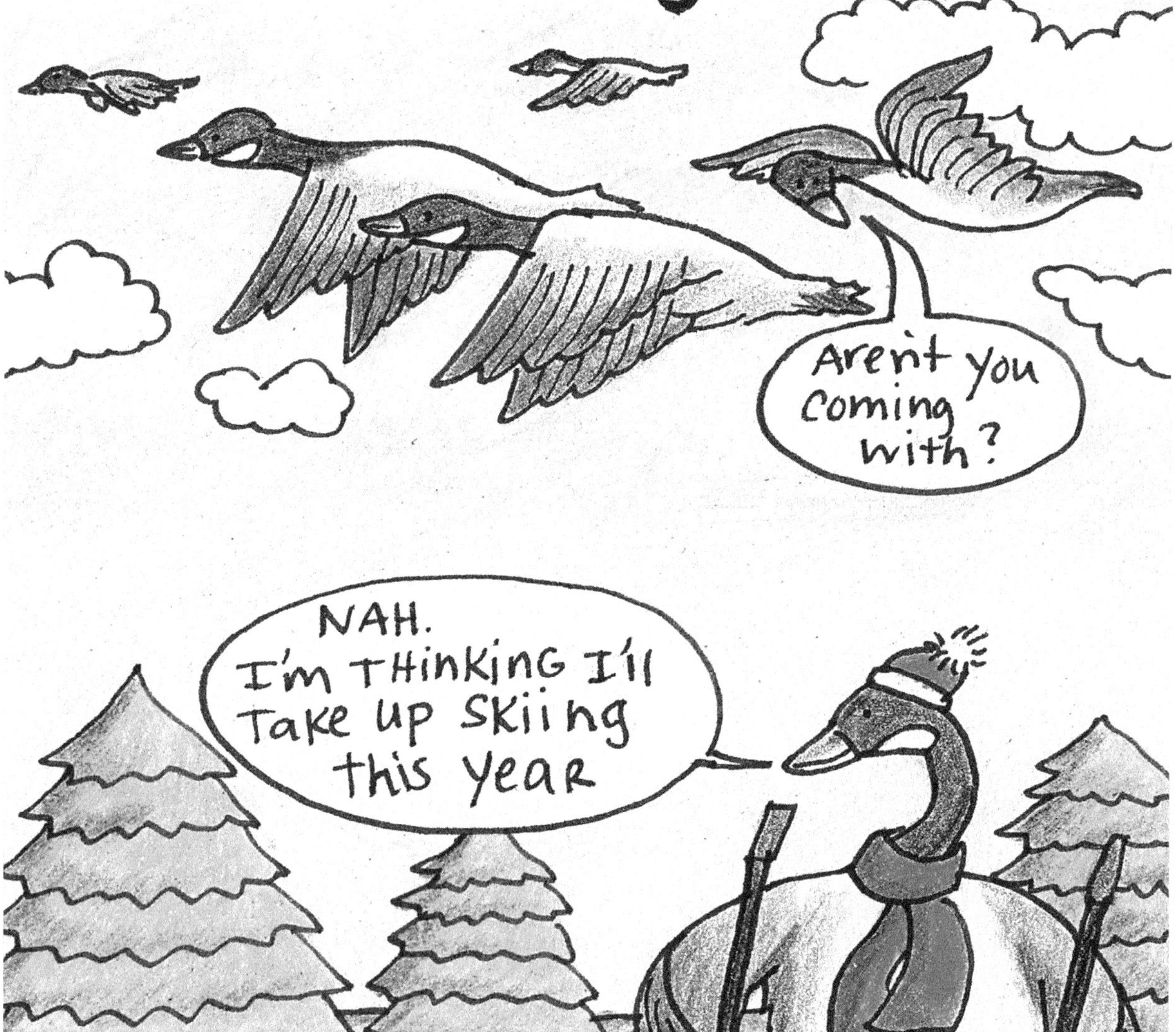

Note #33

Hey, Sweet Girl,

I can't tell you how many times I followed someone else's lead because I didn't know there was a leader in me. Your thoughts are brilliant. Your voice is brilliant. Your ideas are brilliant. Take every opportunity to believe in yourself and stand up for what is important to you. You won't get very far if you are always doing what other people think you should do. Eventually, your bright self will want to shine through, and she will. Get an early start, and from here on in, form your own opinions, believe in your own ideas, and share your unique voice. The world deserves it! What's one way that you can be a leader in your own life today? #theleaderinme

XOXO,
from a girl who gets it

Practice Gratitude

Note #34

Hello, Fascinating Girl,

Being thankful is not something that should only happen on Thanksgiving. It's important to pay attention to all the good things in your life as often as you can!! When we appreciate the things that we already have, more of the good stuff naturally flows into our lives and we will have even more opportunities to feel grateful. How cool is that? Now, I didn't learn about this whole gratitude thing until I was much older, so take it from me, start today and notice all the amazing things around you. You will be amazed at how good it feels to be happy with what's right in front of you instead of focusing all your energy on what you want more of. Let's play the appreciation game. What's one thing in your life you appreciate right now? #gratituderocks

XOXO,

from a girl who gets it

Note #35

Hey, Kind Girl,

Living an awesome life is all about making meaningful connections with the people around you. Just beware, though, sometimes we don't realize that we are sharing things that bring us and our friends down. Sharing private information that someone trusted you with, being a complainer, or saying mean things behind someone's back fall into this category. The only time it's okay to talk behind someone's back is when you are saying something nice about them. Be the person who shares the good news, a good mood, and overall good vibes with the people around you. It's much easier to share the good stuff and it feels great too! The bonus is that when you are a person with a positive outlook, people will want to be around you. That kind of good energy is contagious, after all! How can you share one good thing with someone today? #sharethegoodstuff

XOXO,

from a girl who gets it

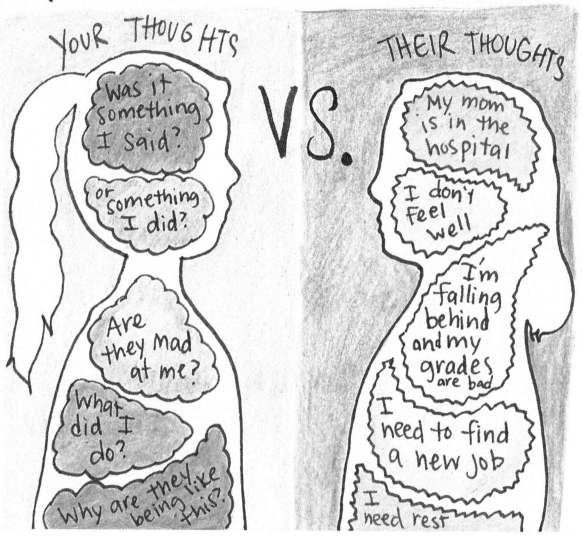

Note #36

Hello, Spectacular Girl,

So I know this may come off a little harsh, but I truly don't mean it to. Just keep reading so you can understand this better. Picture me saying this in the most loving way possible again: not everything is about you. So often someone we love may be quiet, or not all there on a given day, and we will convince ourselves that it is because of something we did or didn't do. The truth is that other people will have their own ups and downs in life, just like we all do, and if you are going to get caught up in trying to figure out how their mood is about you, you will make yourself straight-up crazy! Most times, it will have absolutely nothing at all to do with you. So, take this from me, don't start reading into a situation or making up a story that's not real. Trust that if something involves you, the people involved will share that with you. No guessing games necessary! #itsnotaboutyou

XOXO,

from a girl who gets it

Note #37

Hey, Epic Girl,

Have you ever heard the people who love you say, "Enjoy your life"? Well, they are absolutely right. Let me break it down for you right now. As we've discussed, life has its share of ups and downs. That's part of the flow of being a human being who is having a human experience. The important takeaway here is that you enjoy the good moments, like, a lot. If there is a reason to be sad, be sad, but if not, take comfort and joy in what is going right and don't be afraid to get over the top excited about it too! There's no such thing as jinxing a good moment by enjoying it too much. That's simply ludicrous. In fact, when you celebrate your wins, you get more wins. That's just a universal law. What is going well in your life right now? #celebratenow

XOXO,

from a girl who gets it

Note #38

Hey, Lovable Girl,

Have you ever stopped and asked yourself about your own story? I want you to think of your life as a book. You are the author, creator, decider of all things. Up until this point, what kind of story would you consider your life to be? Drama? Comedy? Horror? Tearjerker? Just like any good author, you can decide what your main character is like and what strengths and gifts she has to get through and grow through life. So take a moment to think about your story so far and decide if it's the one that you actively want to choose for yourself. If not, change it up! After reading this book, you now know that all of the tools you need to be the person that you want are on the inside. From this day on, how will your story continue? #writeagoodstory

XOXO,

from a girl who gets it

Hey, Gorgeous Girl,

Right off the bat, I need you to know and accept that you are beautiful right now. Yes, you are! You don't need to change a thing about yourself to fit in and stand out. The world may try to convince you that a certain body type, eye color, or height is more desirable. Do not listen to that nonsense a minute longer! Get yourself in front of a mirror right now. Look at yourself. You are a perfect creation of the universe, whether or not you realize it yet. You don't have to share it with me if you don't want to, but I ask you to share with yourself one thing you like about your face or body when seeing your reflection in the mirror. Then point that mirror to your heart and share one thing about you that is on the inside that you love. Do this every day, and I promise you will start to feel as beautiful as you are, inside and out! You are your own brand of beautiful. It's as simple as that. What's one thing about you that you know is beautiful? #hellobeautiful

XOXO,

from a girl who gets it

Note #40

Hey, Magnificent Girl,

If you want to be the intelligent girl that we both know you are, it's super important that you make every effort to expand your mind each and every day. What do I mean by this? What I mean is that every minute that passes by is actually giving you the opportunity to be better and stronger than the minute before, so pay attention! Each day, I want you to: find something that challenges you, try something new, be curious, ask questions, and for the love of all that is real, step out of your comfort zone as often as you can. If you're always doing what's easy, you simply won't have the chance to rise up to your full potential. What's one way that you can grow and learn today? #learnandgrow

XOXO,
from a girl who gets it

Note #41

Hello, Spirited Girl,

When I was your age, I used to be so silly in a good way. I spoke in funny accents and created my own hilarious language that all of my friends and family used to adore. Although throughout the years I have lost a little bit of my funny edge, I search for and uncover it as often as I can because that's the real me. The one who doesn't care what other people think and enjoys living in the moment for myself. The gift of me being silly was that other people would feel comfortable enough to be their wackiest, craziest, real-est selves too. The moral of the story here is, don't be afraid to embrace your inner weird. It may not be for everyone, but the ones who get it will be your friends for life, and you will feel good showing what's really inside of you. Trust me, I've been there. Just keep in mind I'm talking about good crazy, the kind where you are still using that beautiful brain to make sure that you are safe while you're having fun. How can you unleash your inner crazy? #getgoodcrazy

XOXO,

from a girl who gets it

Learn to listen

Note #42

Hey, Majestic Girl,

Did you ever notice that if you move around the letters in the word LISTEN, you can actually spell SILENT? There's your first hint right there—we must get silent in order to really (and I mean really) listen to what someone is saying. Now, I know, up until now I've been telling you how important it is to share your voice and own what's real for you, and that's all still very true. But listening is just as important as sharing. When we listen to what someone is saying it doesn't mean that we have to accept and believe in everything that they're saying, but it does mean that A) We can learn some new information, B) We can look at a situation in another way, C) We've made someone feel very special by giving them our undivided attention, D) They will have the same respect for us. So simple, yet sometimes we forget. What opportunity can you take today to truly listen to what someone is saying? #listenup

XOXO,
from a girl who gets it

Drop the comparison game

Fantastic

also Fantastic

Note #43

Hey Amazing Girl!

You know that thing you do...the thing we all do where we look at someone else's life and we count who's got more of this, and who's got less of that, and so on? Feels pretty icky, right? I know it's really, really hard, but I want you to know that it will only make you feel bad and steal all of your joy. It's like taking all of the happiness inside of you and throwing it in the garbage can. Get my point? Instead, accept that we all have this life that has been given to us, along with the power to live and enjoy it in the best way possible. So, the next time you start playing the comparison game, take your eyes off the other person's life and start counting your own blessings. What's one thing in your life that you are super thankful for today? #comparenomore

XOXO,

from a girl who gets it

Expect Miracles

protection in time of need

People changing before your eyes

Healthy family relationships

random acts of kindness

Note #44

Hey, Fabulous Girl,

Did you know that you live in an infinite world that has infinite possibilities? The opportunities for good things to come your way are endless. What we choose to expect of ourselves and the world around us often gets delivered, so wouldn't it be nice to change our expectations for the better? Miracles are actually really small, subtle shifts in us. We need to really be paying attention in life to notice them, and honestly, most of the time a miracle comes from inside of you. It's the willingness to choose to see something in a new way, a way that makes you feel peaceful and better on the inside. I want you to take every opportunity today (and every day) to notice all of the miracles in and around you. What's one miracle that you can think of right now? #miracleseverywhere

XOXO,
from a girl who gets it

Note #45

Greetings, Friendly Girl,

I know, I know, you've heard this one many times before. There is a reason that this message keeps coming up for you, my lovely. It's because you are valuable, and you owe it to yourself (and all of the people around you) to rise to your potential. Success and happiness aren't just going to magically flow into your life. They require some hard work and follow-through. Wishing and waiting isn't going to make your dreams come true, action will. So, you want to become a good cook? Get in the kitchen and start creating. You want good grades? Study hard, girl! You want a group of friends who love you unconditionally? Get out there and be the best friend you can possibly be. Catch my drift? Excellent! What's one thing you are ready to try hard and act big on today? #doyourbest

XOXO,

from a girl who gets it

Note #46

Hey, Smart Girl,

Do you or someone you know ever make things harder than they need to be because you want to get attention or to feel noticed? I want you to really think about it before you respond. I know that I am guilty of this. We all are. When something not so good happens, don't make it worse than it is. When you do that, then finding your way out of the problem and into a solution gets so much harder. Sometimes, we exaggerate for the sake of creating a really good story but that's not cool either because then we are being untruthful. Try to avoid drama—that goes for dramatic people, situations, fake stories—all of it! If you want to feel loved and noticed, do something positive for that attention. The thing with drama is that once you feed it, it follows you around in everything you do. When that happens, it gets harder and harder to avoid it. Stay drama-free, lovely girl! What's one positive way that you can get noticed? #dramafree

XOXO,
from a girl who gets it

Share positive vibes
POSITIVITY
Nice to see you all again! You always brighten our day!
Always a pleasure!

Note #47

Hey, Magnetic Girl,

In any given situation, you get to choose what kind of energy you bring to an experience. When you are in a bad mood or constantly finding things to complain about, you will simply bring more negative experiences into your life. Instead, if you choose to bring your positive vibes to a situation (especially stuff you're not terribly excited about), you can change your own mood and the moods of those around you. Recently my friend and I went into a store where the cashier was a total stick in the mud. We did an experiment where we brought out our own high vibes by joking around with him and singing in the store, and by the end of our shopping experience we were all laughing and feeling good. Talk about an energy shift! How can you bring your high-vibe energy to a situation that needs some positivity? #spreadlove

XOXO,

from a girl who gets it

Note #48

Hey, Awesome Girl,

Trying to make everything happen in your own way and on your own timeline just isn't realistic. If you really think about it, it actually feels kind of uncomfortable to be so controlling. The only person you have true influence over is you guessed it, you! You can't make anyone do what you want them to, be who you want them to, or feel what you want them to feel. You can, however, choose your own actions, behaviors, and responses. And guess what? Even when you do that, you ultimately cannot control the final outcome of every life event, anyway. So, make a promise to yourself right now that instead of controlling, you will always try your best in all situations and let go of your idea of how something should or shouldn't turn out. Believe it or not, most times when you do this, things end up working out even better than you could have hoped for because of your willingness to let go. What situation or person in your life are willing to let go of trying to control? #controlfree

XOXO,

from a girl who gets it

FORGIVE

Her fault

His fault

Their fault

Stop blaming and understand yourself

Take responsibility for your part

Be kind instead of right

Let go and let love

Note #49

Hello, Powerful Girl,

Oh, how I wish I was taught about forgiveness earlier in my life. I used to think that forgiveness means that I am literally saying that it's okay that someone hurt or wronged me. That's not what it is at all. Forgiveness is about letting go of what the other person did so that you could finally have peace in your heart and in your mind. It really doesn't feel good at all to always carry the very heavy weight of disappointment and anger because of something that somebody else did or didn't do. After all, would you rather be right, or would you rather be happy? Being right while being angry doesn't make a whole lot of sense. I hope you will choose happy every time. Stop holding those grudges. Your happiness is waaaaay more valuable than that. My promise to you is that once you have truly forgiven, you will feel so free and clear. What situation or person are you willing to forgive? #forgivenessheals

XOXO,

from a girl who gets it

Hi, Visionary Girl,

By now I'm pretty certain that you already know this, but just in case there is still any doubt at all, I want you to know that everything is going to be okay. More likely, everything is going to be great. You know why? Yeah, you do. Because it's all inside of you. All the power, all the confidence, and all the strength you need to bravely live your life already exist in your big, beautiful heart. Now is your time to do your thing and simply be the girl that you want to be and now know that you can be. Take it from me, I've been there, I've already gone through all of this and more, and I totally get it. #itsallgood

XOXO,

from a girl who gets it

Book Club Questions

What's one way that you can grow from the messages in this book?

How have your thoughts shaped your life so far?

How much choice do you have over the events of your life?

What are some of your unique superpowers?

How can practicing gratitude change your life?

What have you learned from your own inner voice of knowing?

About the Author

Melody Pourmoradi has been coaching women for over a decade on how to create a vision for their best life. She thrives on sharing her message of self-empowerment and a wellness-centered living through her writing. As the creator of the GiRLiFE Empowerment Series, she has created a digital course that teaches women how to create income generating girls empowerment groups in their own communities. Her greatest goal is for every young girl and women to find her own voice and live a life that lights her up from the inside-out. Melody is married to the love of her life and together they are the proud parents of twin girls.

For more information, please visit: www.lifeevolutionscoaching.com, and join the social media conversation on @GiRLiFEempowerment & @life_evolutions.

CPSIA information can be obtained
at www.ICGtesting.com
Printed in the USA
BVHW02*1804200818
524304BV00002BA/2/P

9 781732 098008